SKIRTED

SKIRTED

poems

Julie Marie Wade

THE WORD WORKS
WASHINGTON, D.C.

Skirted © 2021 Julie Marie Wade

Reproduction of any part of this book in any form or by any means, electronic or mechanical, except when quoted in part for the purpose of review, must be with permission in writing from the publisher. Address inquiries to:

THE WORD WORKS
P.O. Box 42164
Washington, D.C. 20015
editor@wordworksbooks.org

Cover design: Susan Pearce

LCCN: 2021930387
ISBN: 978-1-944585-47-1

Acknowledgments

With gratitude to the editors of the following, in which these poems appear:

Anti-Poetry: "I'm drowning here, & you're describing the water." & "There's no hole on earth where the heart drops through without bringing something with it."
Carousel: "Détente"
Cerise Press: "What Nimrod Should Have Known"
Cream City Review: "The Cartographer"
Cutthroat: "Peripeteia" & "Prelude (What I Wish Had Happened)"
Dogwood: "Love Poem for Sisyphus"
Dos Passos Review: "Empathy for Electra"
Drunken Boat: "The Generalist" & "The Opaque Dilemma of Daylight"
Green Mountains Review: "Fallout"
kill author: "Or else."
Nimrod: "Requiem for the White Bluff Watch Dog"
Notre Dame Review: "The Fire-Eater"
Open 24 Hours: "The Follower"
Pebble Lake Review: "Roanoke"
Phoebe: "Law of Parsimony"
Scrivener Creative Review: "Pangaea," "Pangaea (2)," "Pangea (3)," "Pangaea (4)," & "Pangaea (5)"
Spoon River Poetry Review: "Ekphrasis" & "Source Amnesia"
Theodate: "Double Feature"
Tupelo Press Poetry Project: "We Leave the Beaches for the Tourists, Mostly"
The West Review: "Lake Effect"

Marie Alexander Flash Sequence Anthology: ("I'm drowning here, & you're describing the water.," "Or else," "Skirt the issue.," "There's no hole on earth where the heart drops through without bringing something with it.," "You can't marry someone when you're in love with someone else.")

A number of poems included here were first published in *Without*, a selection of the New Women's Voices Chapbook Series, Finishing Line Press, 2010.

The poem "Lake Effect" was adapted for string quartet and mezzo soprano by composer James Young; it was first performed at the Comstock Concert Hall (Louisville, Kentucky) on November 20, 2008.

The title "I'm drowning here, & you're describing the water." is a line borrowed from the 1997 film *As Good As It Gets*.

The title "There's no hole on earth where the heart drops through without bringing something with it." is a line borrowed from the 2008 poetry collection *Now You're the Enemy*, by James Allen Hall.

The title "You can't marry someone when you're in love with someone else." is a line borrowed from the 1965 film *The Sound of Music*.

Thank you to Nancy White and The Word Works Press for publishing *Skirted*, the folio formerly known as D R IF T. You saw the "if" in it, and under your guidance, a conditional manuscript became an actual, hold-in-my-hands-lovely book!

Thank you to Tamiko Beyer, Rajiv Mohabir, and Stephanie Strickland, three writers whose work I have long admired, for lending your voices in support of this project.

Skirted owes a special debt to my Pittsburgh people, as so many of these poems are set there. I feel lucky to have landed in the City of Bridges during such a transformative time in my life and grateful to have crossed those bridges toward you: Amy Patterson, John Miller, Connie Angermeier, Kathryn Flannery, Lucy Fischer, Stacey Waite, Helena Rho, Jeffrey Weise, and the late (and indeed great) Robyn Dawes.

Thank you to my colleagues and students in the creative writing program at Florida International University for these first nine years together and the many more to come.

Abundant gratitude always to Anna Rhodes, Dana Anderson, Tom Campbell, James Allen Hall, Annette Allen, Catherine Fosl, Denise Duhamel, John Dufresne, and my incomparable "Outlaws"—Kim, Matt, Evie, Nolan ("Super Hondo"), and Sam Striegel.

And to Angie Griffin, my forever-person, who has traveled with me from one coast to another, forging this beautiful life we live by the sea. In writing, I often look back. Because of you, I always look forward.

for Angie

then   now   always

Contents

Prelude (What I Wish Had Happened)   13

Pangaea   17
"I'm drowning here, & you're describing the water."   19
The Understudy   21
Empathy for Electra   22
Source Amnesia   23
Ekphrasis   28
Fallout   30

Pangaea (2)   35
What Nimrod Should Have Known   37
"Or else."   38
The Fire-Eater   39
Peripeteia   41
A Posteriori   43
Lake Effect   46

Pangaea (3)   49
The Generalist   51
The Actuary   53
Law of Parsimony   54
"You can't marry someone when you're in love with someone else."   57
Double Feature   59
Love Poem for Sisyphus   61

Pangaea (4)   65
Roanoke   67
Démarche   68
We Leave the Beaches for the Tourists, Mostly   69
The Follower   70
"Skirt the issue."   72
Wane   73

Pangaea (5) 79
The Opaque Dilemma of Daylight 81
The Cartographer 83
Requiem for the White Bluff Watch Dog 84
Détente 85
Reading Robinson Crusoe Again, for the Last Time 86
"There's no hole on earth where the heart drops through
 without bringing something with it." 88

Prelude (What I Wish Had Happened)

That the sea had risen in sudden fury—
over the bulkheads lacy with moss,
rough with barnacles & bits of shell;
over the slippery rocks & the dark
trenches of sand pocked by clams
still breathing beneath them; over
even the splintered, lice-ridden logs.
Then, with the vigor of something
like love—over the promenades also
& the footpaths arcing into the woods,
over the ballfields with their broken
fences & the battered Poison Ivy signs.

That the sea had kept rising through
the city park, its horseshoe pit shaded
by lilacs, its swing sets ancient &
loosely hinged. That it had flowed
onto Fauntleroy Way in time with
the evening rush; that the row of cars
waiting for their ferry ride home
were left bobbing there, chrome
buoys in a salt-drenched storm.

That the sea, which I had always known
was coming for me, came at last—
gliding over concrete; scaling
the grassy banks with its liquid fingers;
pouring through the latticework of
the red gate that separated our yard
from all the others; then rising to the
height of the picture windows where I
picture my parents still: together
winding their grandfather clock, slashing
each square on the calendar.
Which is to say—sad, without
knowing they are sad, frightened of
time moving & time standing still.

This sea will fracture that glass, & with it,
the tiny, treacherous globe of all my past
lives, even the old paperweight world
resting on the desk, smoothed with felt on
the underside to keep it from slipping away.
Of this I am certain: what we can't stop, in the
end, we destroy. But if, miraculous & auspicious,
a flood begins, like the hired gun of the heart's
truest intention, we surrender everything—
merchandise & misgivings, the old
grudge & the ensuing plan, until even
the baby grand is newly repurposed,
a boat seeping its soggy music, tender &
futile against the faithless white spume.

Obliteration, we say; *or a new beginning.*

"I made no voyages, I owned no passport.
I was the daughter."

—Anne Sexton

Pangaea

These continents—

    land   or   sleep   or   snow

        (things that drift, that deepen)

And the nets of the heart cast wide across the ever-widening sea

    (Ts'ai Ken T'an)   *Water which is too pure has no fish.*

No danger here: purity   prescience   grace

        (things that are promised, that do not appear)

For my mother, one indisputable truth—

    how men & women are meant to cleave:

    the sheaves of their bodies bundled

weltered re-enactment of Adam & Eve

    (John H. Miller) *For the more romantic among you, assume*
        a stained glass window.

What of mosaic then, what of pastiche?

Planchette of the body gliding: syllable,   sound

(things that are known beyond language)

"I'm drowning here, & you're describing the water."

The water is lush & cool. The water consists of fishes with vermillion eyes & scuba divers seeking recompense for stolen treasure. The water will not wait. The water is not accustomed to waiting. The water understands (implicitly) that you are afraid. The water will forgive your tremors, your flails, but is not interested in negotiating your fears. The water speaks (explicitly) in waves. The water dashes many dreams to stone. The water harbors many stones as dreams. The water remains complicit, clouded, circumspect: equal parts wavering & unwavering. The water enjoys an occasional play on words. The water will not laugh & cannot stop crying. The water is at once stoic & superfluous where emotions are concerned. The water regards the moon coldly. The water is a breeding ground for science fiction. The water swallows trashy romance novels & family-sized umbrellas. The water contains a silverware drawer replete with spoons. The water is specialized in ontology, epidemiology, & acrobatics. The water also knows something (implicitly) about tautology, effervescence, & ravines. The water taxes for occupancy per diem. The water simulates envelopes & epithets, unfolding & dispensing. The water rarely engages in debate concerning justice, light, the vitality of sand, the accoutrement of shells, or the significance of sailing. The water understands you do not understand. The water will not wait after all. The water is not accustomed to waiting. The water is weak & warm. The water is controlled by invisible currents that mimic gravity but cannot replicate it. The water is different every time. The water separates (explicitly) driftwood from other kinds of logs. The water composes symphonies, performs operas. The water dictates to an imaginary amanuensis on the shore. The water would like to be kind. The water is not sure how to be kind. The water swallows patchwork blankets & beach towels. The water is stricken with grief but has never learned precisely how to mourn. The water is specialized in sinking. The water remains pent, pickled, prone: equal parts willing & unwilling. The water would like you to enter. The water would like you to feel comfortable but is not interested in elaborate gestures of attenuation. The water is shy & struggles with salutations. The water fears itself unremarkable. The water bellows when it means to inquire. The water suggests you have had a hard day & should take off your shoes. The water has already eaten. The water exists in tenuous relation to voyeurism & seduction: those cult-followers in the ring-side seats. The water hopes you will not judge the water prematurely. The water hopes you are able to stay awhile. The water would be happy to fix you a drink. The water once wrote a lyric poem called "Capsize," which was recited near a lighthouse in Bar Harbor. The water remembers when you were a child, remembers it fondly. The water keeps your pink jelly-shoes for posterity. The water is novice & ageless & lost. The water rebukes cliffs & renounces valleys. The water understands the pressure is always changing. The water wishes you would step back a little. The water is concerned with catachresis, though it has never uttered the word. The water is the strong, silent type. The water has a lava lamp in place of a heart. The water regrets it is unable to lunch today. The water desires your presence at a future event. The water blushes & rushes over your toes. Thank you, the water says. Thank you for listening.

The Understudy

Imagine how it must have seemed to her: understudy of her own life,
still husked in the childhood body, still cinched at the waist with an assortment
of safety belts & one fabric leash the nanny snapped to her back
as they went out about the neighborhood.

Imagine the latticed fences & the padlocked gates & the patchwork quilt
beneath which her long, exuberant torso could be found crumpled & curled,
late nights with a flashlight, a playbook, & a bowl of pitted cherries.
She must have loved *Our Town* best, with its attention to the clandestine,
the nostalgic, & the lost. She was the kind of girl, the kind of Emily, who could
render a line
like "The moonlight's so terrible" more real than even Wilder had intended.

In fact, it must have been terrible—all that moon-bathing through the attic transoms
as night after night she failed to succumb to sleep. In the morning, instead of
waking, she simply rose—pale as gaslight & pink about the eyes from hours
hunched & squinting into the amorous, gallant, withholding dark of her most
nubile imagination.

In this way, imagine how she surprised herself with longing—tenderfoot tempted
by the briar-patch, harp-string calluses on her fingertips, candle wax dripping
salaciously into her navel & the hollow backs of her knees. Any moment,
she thought, the stage might appear in all its transcendent glory.
Roses might manifest on the mahogany tables & the varnished windowsills,
as if ravaged from some prelapsarian garden, that rough & wild look about them:
no longer prop-like, their smooth & naked stems.

And the Mother & Father who lived also in the house would pose there
on the proscenium, one to Stage Right & one to Stage Left, the first draped in a
sable coat, the second smoking a pipe & staring blankly toward the future.
Some Joan Crawford type, some Peter Lorre... As if biology had never bound them
with its cord & knot; as if the dowry chest in the crawlspace below the kitchen stairs
did not contain something—anything—she might have wanted; as if the tiny
ballerina in the jewel box were only an artifact of another time & not, more precisely,
a version of herself in miniature, becoming the pirouette into which her body turned.

Empathy for Electra

who was not easy   that ganglion
of a girl   axon-smooth &   dendrite-
scattered   cleft nerves of neural
illusion   something in us always
favors revenge   a line drawn
then crossed   transversals of mischief
& myelin

as myth renders the meaning secondary
to the source   so also   the primary
lust the primitive passion   for all that
Mother & Father   could not give
& for what it would mean to live
without them

be it heart   or be it brave cerebellum
that bears the burden of balancing
between extremes   (& maybe she did
leave Mycenae at the wrong moment (&
maybe yes her path was brambled
whether or not their own was bent

but there's a place in the palm where the
life-line drops off & the tines of the line
are revenge)   or remorse)   or regret)

who could fault her the years of falter?
with her butterfly net & her wishing-you-wells
who could fault her   that salty air
those meager coins   plumbing an ancient pause:
wanting them back   or was it
wanting them *new*?

Source Amnesia

The day has come, your mother has forgotten.
Your father tries to remember,
but she erases him also, so the pages of his
knowing are torn clean through, like the
garments of a prophet transfigured.

Your mother resolves this arbitrary hour,
on this ordinary summer day, that you are
worth more to her elapsed than alive—
a figment now, a figure no longer.

Meanwhile, in an airport lavatory,
you scrub your hands.
Meanwhile.
A soft word.
Essential, luxurious
as soap.

Your mother is disgusted. The thought
of you touching a woman disgusts her so
deeply she can think of little else. But now
when she thinks of you, it is like gazing
at the smashed fist of a broken mirror—
its spider webs of glass—unable to admit
reflection.

Two skeletons—faceless, fleshless—
knocking bones beneath translucent sheets.

Your father browses dime stores, delays
his return to the brick bunker-house on the
seaside lane.

If only he could remember:
the special significance of the colored tags,
how much off today, how much tomorrow.

It is not the way she imagines. *You* are not
the way.   Still, the mounting alarm
after all these years—reeled back in, cast &
re-cast in the long pantomime of
her disappointment.   And when you look
over your shoulder in the bathroom mirror,
there is no one visible, no one who would let
herself be seen.

Meanwhile, your father continues
to mean well—his intentions
useful & robust
as a fist against
a concrete door.

On the small perishable province between
innocence & guilt, you have woven
your nest, stitched up your solitude, begun—
if only *begun*—to lower the louvered blinds
of your heart.

Loathing is easy, obvious,
but the essential luxury—indifference:
to begin—if only begin—to turn a cold
shoulder to the non-figure whose breath
steams slow flowers up the glass.

Meanwhile. The woman who touches
your freshly washed hands is nothing
like your mother. Thank God for that.
Thank God.

Your father: contusion of aimless love,
Protestant ambition. Praise God for the woman
who sews his pockets shut, seals the portal
to temptation.

O, for the change slipping through,
the linty sourballs!

O, for what threatens to pass!

Some arbitrary hour of this ordinary
summer a woman is washing clothes—
washing them & hanging them out to dry.

You may recognize her as your mother;
you may not.

In the end, it makes no difference.
She will not recognize you.

Outside in the morning chill, she pins
each garment to the wire tree, shrill bird
tilting on its rusting axis.

The pockets of her apron bulge with wooden pegs.
The shoulders of her blouses rise with yeast of cushions.

In this light, she is not beautiful—
not even a little—
but you wish you could love her
just the same.

Meanwhile.

Your father wanders through parking lots.
Your lover lingers near the refreshment stand.

You have choked back everything
human: terror, honor, tears.
But now maybe you would if you could:
would meet her face to face—casualties
of the broken light, calluses on time's
ancient weary heels—

Instead, you turn your palms upward
under the low heat, wiggle your ten
good fingers on your two strong hands,

consider the blessing of skin: the skiff of
her breath, the wave of your flesh—
gratitude, lust, compassion.

So you leave a room with a faucet
for another without one, knowing a faucet is
a valuable thing, knowing you take nothing
if not your own life in your hands.

On the small perishable province
between restoration & regret,
a body still bows, still bends:

Be it a sink, or a spigot, or
a wild spring—

        you see her clearly: there,
        always: that stranger—she, you—
        kneeling now, washing her hands.

Ekphrasis

If there had been a moment of knowing,
unalterably, who I was & who I was
intended (predestined?) to love—a prophesy
of some sort, Calvinist rigor & Catholic grace,
wherein the riddles of longing were solved—once & for all—
it would have been that moment, with my father,
at the beachfront art shop in Seaside, Oregon.

Perhaps he had his own dreams, unpleasantly parsed
into discrete compartments, arranged around a card table of
dogs playing poker, confirmed again in the elegiac eyes of Marilyn Monroe,
gazing back at him from the bathroom wall.

Together we wandered into the tentative warmth of midday, past
cabanas & cafes & the carousel spinning in perpetuity (indeterminancy?) until
we found our way into a gallery, with Easter egg walls & Christmas tree lights
& the fantasy that mere brightness could substitute
for class or quality.

Then, the moment... mythical though it must be, & rendered without speech:
only a small gasp caught in the throat,
like a fist after a blow (the knuckles shattered)...
I did not inhabit my body then. I never had. Yet there I was, plummeting
      suddenly
from the hot air balloon of arboreal attention, aerial dimension—
into my skin, all the way in—
to the physicality I had spent a lifetime fighting.
And this was the light at last.

Coastline. Painted by Steve Hanks in 1989. A fusion of those creations most
beautiful to me—women & the sea. No, I had never thought of it before—
that combination—though I had been troubled by a certain restless urgency
... and then this calm (peace?), as if the painting already knew all about me
& understood, implicitly, that to desire these things was good, & no less
natural than to desire the hard surface of land, the bristled bodies of men.

But water, in the end, is where we come from, & the woman
with her back to the lens of our looking—with her narrow shoulders pert as fins,
with her posture neither wistful nor regretting—demands in fact
that we follow her gaze out across the vastness of the landscape—
as if to say, *Yes, I have lured you here*; as if to say, *No, you are not permitted escape.*

I was mesmerized by this, & more than this: by the desire to occupy not just
    my own body
but also hers, & not in the vicarious or ephemeral sense, but deeply,
    deliberately: that difference so keen
between being like and being with—admiration or attraction—& despite this false
dichotomy, I could not have been more certain that my yearning was of the
    second nature
& not the first, & that my hunger was not merely virginal but visceral:
lightning yet to be loosed . . .

My father came & stood beside me, & I could see him
tracing the line of her with his eyes, roving the white dress & the faintly visible
curve of the thighs
beneath it, & the slender arms & the tousled hair
& then that cowed feeling encroaching again—as if he wondered how a lone body
set against a backdrop of rock & shell could cast such a spell, could remind him
again of what his own life had been lacking:
something fierce & elemental & ultimately uncontained.

I stood with my father: never closer, never farther.
We lusted together in the same way.

Fallout

Radioactive decay is the set of various processes by which unstable atomic nuclei (nuclides) emit subatomic particles. Decay is said to occur in the parent nucleus and to produce a daughter nucleus.

Allegory made easy, our story foreshadowed by science:
another nuclear family destined for disintegration.

But we want to be special, don't we? We want
to believe in the mercurial majesty of our own

destruction. Even now, all these miles away,
I take refuge in cool subjunctive caves:

If only I believed more avidly in God…
If only I had kept the Fourth Commandment…

My mother had a plan. She told me to stay at home
till I was 30, live in her basement, borrow her car.

I could take the bus to school in the University District,
complete my Ph.D. without the desperate quest

for money, without acquiring a single pint of debt.
My father agreed. It only made sense. And then,

by their unanimous decree, I would be married, & a down
payment would be waiting for me on a three-

bedroom brick rambler in their water-view community—
close by, so they could always watch the children.

That birthright was wealth & security, secret sex &
cigarettes stubbed out beneath the wide camellia tree

that obscured my bedroom window all those years.
It was my mother screaming, for reasons unbeknownst

to science, my father pledging his fleeting remedy:
Whatever you want, Darling. Whatever you need.

So we come back again to detritus, the cells
of appeasement & displeasure sloughing off my skin

until I glimpsed the mannequin of their most ample
aspirations, that proxy-woman I could not become.

My father said: "You're killing your mother."
My mother said: "Listen to your father."

But I had a sundial & a strong intuition &
that sinking-ship feeling that shook me clean

to my soles. We were headed for a capsize,
my family & I, evoking words like asunder

& adrift. "Are you trying to be an outcast?"
my mother asked, which only begged the question:

cast out of what? A house of order—built on
stilts, perched in sand? Secret society of

private misgivings & public thanksgivings?
There's what we say, & what we do,

then there's what we breathe: whole climate
committed to asphyxiation, slow

incineration of a last honest wish,
final non-bureaucrat's desire.

I can hold my breath a long time under water,
my swimmer's lungs primed for intervals

of deep submersion. But I can't open my eyes.
It's a problem of underworld survival,

learning the way of touch, calculated kinesthesia
through a wilderness of stray sounds, refracted

lights. Here beneath the surface of things,
where the floating debris cannot reach me,

I still feel the earthly tremors, voices booming,
searchlights probing these depths.

Pangaea (2)

In dreams   how easily   I shed my skin

un-tethered: Gender's ridged tail

mermaid   merman

(creature for which no name, no form)

I am she: I am he

And the wreck   of silence   sinking   sleep

bears no resemblance to that mythic Ark

2 x 2 x 2 x 2 x 2 x 2 x 2

We are, I am, you are

all breath   all blood   all bone

Ice over the Erie Lake suddenly broken through

neither I nor you

broke

nor

breaker

Treatise of tongues without rupture

floe/flow

the evidence of damage

brokered

flowered

no light at the surface   sonorous abyss

I go down   *Love*   *I go down*

What Nimrod Should Have Known

The word
        like wood
is porous & prone
        to sliver
The tongue
        which is called *mother*
answers to a hundred
        other names
The stutterer
        child of slow illocution
of swift permutation
        utters an equivalent truth
Even wrapped in
        Eve's garments
even wielding the sword of
        Adam's violent vernacular
The Jenga puzzle of speech
        totters, glottal-stopped
in the throat of
        forthcoming & *forgotten*
On the lips of the
        blotted horizon
where *eminent* & *imminent*
        splinter into reef & wave
And the twin pillars
        of the crushed tower
jut forth from the sea: one boasting
        Silence, the other *Cacophony*.

"Or else."

Fabled ending or outcome. Epilogue of *what if?* & *then what?* & *why not?* Caprice's cornerstone. Threat's conviction. Frontispiece (or) shield. Dorsal (or) ventral. That-which-is-left-dangling. If I cast my nets wide, will I catch you? If I hunker down, shiny amphibian in the slick wetland grasses, will I strike & will someone else yield? There is this other about it, this "other" & this furtive "othering." What happens is…& no one knows how to answer, but we know it's wrong; we understand that we are meant to be afraid, outraged, indignant. Rubble loosens at the precipice. Ascend at your own risk. *Falling Rocks*. If I jump off a bridge, will you follow? If I leap from a tree with a frayed rope wrapped over & under my glistening naked splendor, will we collide inside the shallow water? Is collision ever a good thing? What happens is…& no one knows how to answer, but we know it's light- & ache-filled, eyes straining to see as through fog. Your guiding hand through a white subversive darkness. Something on the other side? Dorsal? Ventral? Switch, flip, turn. There is this other about it, this "other" & this furtive "othering." We don't know for sure what frightens us, but leave a light on in the closet please & a note inside the lunchbox that promises forgiveness or reprieve. If a tree falls in a forest, is it *indicative* of error? If I am watching from the landing of a tree house, Rima-like—bird-girl cloaked in leaves & trepidation—does my vision validate or overwrite the scene? What happens is…& no one knows how to answer, but we know it's cold & sweat-streaked & libidinous: what only some are entitled to feel. Caprice's cornerstone. Threat's conviction. Is the promise (always) punishment? Is the captor (ever) kind? Futures as elusive as storybook rhymes: shoes that fit because they're forced to, because they *must*. If I discover I am not "just like" my neighbor, will I be forced to resign our common garden? If I lean in close to the window that marks us separate, delineates our heterogeneous zones, am I inviting a similar prurience to that which I seek to extract? There is this other about it, this "other" & this furtive "othering." Frontispiece (or) shield. Dorsal (or) ventral. The chiming of a grandfather clock. The keeping of tide schedules. One eye bent on the moon. What happens is…& no one knows how to answer, but we know it's always with us—need or demand—three-way contingency or contractual agreement. Two steps forward, another back. That-which-is-always-left-dangling.

The Fire-Eater

Childhood: parade
of blazing torches, scorched
pillows, smoke & mirrors.

You go to the light show.
That woman is there—
the anchor from television.

Your mother says you could be
smart & attractive just like her,
when you grow up, *if*.

Cigarettes may stunt your growth.
Another episode of *Highway to Heaven*
for moral support. Angels, it seems,

really are "above it all." And see how
caffeine makes the frog's exposed
heart beat harder. Coffee will stain

your teeth. And Sun-In will turn your
hair orange. The best pets are chameleons.
(The best people, too.)

You like the scent of cloves.
You lick the sweet paper before
placing the dark stick in your mouth.

The best kisses taste like cloves.
The best stoves have pilot lights
that never waver. The best pilots

have perfect night vision. Headlights
will only get them so far. The joint is
communal. You pass it around.

"Are you having a good trip?" Someone
wants to know. Someone's living room is
warm as Malibu. Someone's hair is white

as corn. How fast the French braid becomes
the French kiss becomes Someone's Father's
exotic brandy with the green vine

growing up, growing if: perpetual possibilities,
liquor-soaked pears. And the bottle spinning,
& the ashes flicking, & the false performance

of freedom that garners quarters on corners
like mediocre mimes
when everyone has time—

tap the pack, strike the match—
time:
to suck   blow   be bothered.

Peripeteia

It's like being 18 again,
the way you can only listen to
so much soft music in a dimly lit room
before something has to perforate or puncture.

the needle stick, or unstick

Your heart a feathered thing,
a quilled, willful thing—*porcupine heart*—
ferocious & abysmal, desperate to pierce
someone else's skin in order to dull its own pain.

So you say to the man you don't love yet
 (may never love, though you know you're supposed to…),
 breath thick in the throat of the body you don't love yet
(may never love, aren't even supposed to…)

"Will you go down to the vending machine?
Will you bring back all the chocolate & a Cherry Coke, too?"
He says, "Now? Right now?" Sweaty at the nape of his neck &
worried, wanting to please you the way candy would, the way caffeine.

is this a test? is this only a test?

So when he's gone in his stocking feet &
the radiator is burning hot like the coals in your father's
old Kamado pot & you are without your buttons & your best sense,
the bobby pins your mother taught you to twist in your hair—*disheveled,*

she might call you now—but remembering a storybook
where the princess took bed sheets & tied them together, descended
the trellis fashioned from the remnants of her *coitus interruptus,*
        into the night,
into the more-than-night of the equinox, onto a road half-paved &
        entirely abandoned.

Are you that woman? Will you be that woman once
or in perpetuity—her ankles shackled to the last outpost of moonlight
on the last path that leads to a lake without a boat ramp—a *Last Summer
    at Bluefish Cove*—
which is where you're headed anyway, whether you know it or not.

a tremor, like someone turned the snow globe over

You hear him knocking. "You locked me out!" he'll say.
You don't answer. His shoes dangle from the telephone line. A prank,
a small amusement to pass the time. "Let me in! Let me in!" he'll say, his voice
growing louder like the Wolf in another story you read,
once upon a time, before bed.

But you deal in riddles now. Even fables are far too long to recount.
You slip a note, perforated, under the door. That quill heart still good for
    something after all.

A Posteriori

then you realize
        you could have been anyone
           (even a human being)

                    & it changes again

the first librarian with the first shush on her lips, wagging an irate finger

                                  vehemence:
                they didn't want you to know about this

        the kaleidoscope
          then the cap gun
          the Magic-8 Ball
       & Barbie's glow-in-the-dark canopy bed

    lemon tree very pretty

                    skipping stones along the seashore
                        just a stone's throw away

          << first the cast stone >>   << stone the first cast >>

theatrics:
they didn't want you to know about these

            but punctuation—   building the pauses in

    phonics— sounding them out, hearing the click between syllables
                      when they all fit together just so

& the lemon flower is sweet

                    Nancy Drew & Holly Golightly
                    Mint Meltaways by the carton
                    an artificial Christmas tree
                    & out-till-ten roller-skating party

stoning
getting stoned
stone-cold

                    << cast the first stone >>

you could have kissed her. . .   you could have fallen. . .
                              Mt. St. Helen's erupting again. . .

the house is made of glass
        the body is made of glass
                the heart is made of glass
                      & the sand it goes without saying

        is made of tiny hearts & bodies & houses—

each of them in various states of shatter

                        but the fruit of the poor lemon

    the   first spelling bee with the first mind-bending word,
                                                      wrapping around the microphone

                      transgression:
                      they didn't want you to know about this

                                        turning to stone
                                        a rolling stone gathers no moss

    << rock & a hard place >>   << hard place & a rock >>

              the +++++++++++
          then the --------------
                the ##########
        & ????????????

you have lazy-eye blindness / you have eyes in the back of your head /
                                      you live a life of quiet voyeurism

        is a thing one cannot eat

then you realize

            you are no one
              (& never have been)

                            as such, you have nothing to lose

Lake Effect

No one warned us about the snowsquall.
Leaving Pittsburgh in the sometime-after-dusk,
our pilgrimage: Nashville before dawn.

Then the snows struck, Ohio bleakening to
blizzard, the highway skirted with
stoic trees, & these—clamped in chains of icy silver.

Part of me wanted to turn back, the night peeling
off in great white sheets, our company of wayfarers
declining at rest stops & coffee shops,

succumbing to the season's incumbent storm.
But we pushed forward: for the holidays, for the family
waiting to greet us, then pretend we had never been born.

And as the world iced over slowly, as the road unfolded before us
only to rescind its kindness—to shimmer the unspoken malice
of a deep & interminable freeze—I thanked the landscape

for its insight, foreshadowing our future: how we could make
the clouds roll in with a single crooked gesture; how we could kiss
& shatter the crystalline skies. And how, above all, we dared

not ask for affirmation, or the faces like garden statues once
rimmed with leaves & birds would crack & jaundice, the
whole gathering of merry angels shrivel & dash to stone.

Pangaea (3)

>>>The look of things has changed.

>>I remember this landscape
>>smaller: brittle & self-contained.

>(Tulip border.) (Invisible fence.) (Sea-wrack skirting the shore.)

>>"What are you looking for?" my father calls.
>>Always with the rocks, overturning.

My mother wanted a gazebo but settled for a swimming pool.

>"Safe water. No tides."
She hadn't counted on the moon's grand omniscience, gravitational charge.

She hadn't counted on me, in my distended mind, all hours of the night—
>>>skinny-dipping.

>>>What I learned there:
>>>what I have struggled most
>>>to forget: the mandate:
>>>*ask permission for your happiness.*

Always with the rocks, overturning.

>>*What may be offered may also be denied.*

>>A calculated moment under mistletoe
>>My gold dress in the moonlight, my terrified glow.

(Shawls across shoulders.) (Invisible fence.) (Electric seatbelt snapping me back.)

Is it any wonder, when I dreamed there, even those wires were tapped?
                    All night their shadowed forms—eavesdropping

    my cerebral chatter, my unconscious wish.

Is it any wonder I began to live in code, desire disguised beyond recognition?

        How many nights, the Woman & Man: their bodies in a flowering hea

    Those hothouse dreams & my humid heart:

where I was not She   but He.

The Generalist

At first, pain is only a hypothesis.
You whisper words in your sleep
you will not pronounce upon waking—

ignominy, epidemiology

You think you have been mostly
really hungry. Mornings after sodium-
rich foods, your mouth sweats instead of thirsts—

cravings, curses

You once made the mistake of believing
you were a specialist. "What makes you
so Goddamn special?" someone asked—

delusions, grandeur

You did not have an answer for that question.

Now a few of these theories have been tested.
A feminist in your spare time, you call them
"theories of the flesh" & try not to hold your tongue—

bodies, burdens

You realize all human beings look essentially
alike. Victims blame themselves, & perpetrators
claim power. The lines between them are oblique at best—

objection, abjection

Words also begin to sound the same.

A number of controversies exist concerning inoculation.
Someone swabs your tender flesh with cotton. A shot. Got it.
The critics want to be helpful but can't stop drawing blood—

    platelets, plasma

You tell yourself not to worry about varicose veins.
No body is perfect. No body knows everything.
The grocery store activates your tear glands—

    salt, water

It saddens you to think you are no exception. Further,
you resent the lack of rules. You suffer no unique psychic damage.
Your pain is neither predictable nor exceptional—

    standard, deviation

You do not have a question for that answer.

The Actuary

is very clear. He does not "deal in the afterlife." If you want a fortune, he suggests a crispy cookie. Palms are tall trees dispensing coconuts, not predictors of anyone's fate. I, on the other hand, am deeply concerned about kismet. And when the mind thinks about the brain which is really the site of the mind thinking, is that akin to the snake eating its own tail? *Chew on this*. Now, a Trident commercial creeps in, & it does actually give you the creeps that there is no firewall for these synaptic sparks. Now, *Mentos fresh & full of life* & back again to the body, to the moment at hand, where love is more than a match of tennis and war is hardly a game. Yet we have this problem with names. Is there a shortage of words, some reason we should turn back to overlapping? When it stopped raining in Seattle, my father said it was like the sun stopped shining in California, only he didn't say it quite that way. Instead, he said, *Californ-I-A*. He was trying to be funny, but it came out sad & strained, as if someone had dried out the plum of his heart & left him in heat to prune. I asked the Actuary, "What are my odds of finishing this poem?" He said he preferred to "operate in concrete numbers." I asked the Actuary, "What are my chances of surviving East Coast winters & this long season of obscurity that wears on me like a tiresome robe?" He said he would "get back to me," sometime after the first of the year. When it stopped snowing in Pittsburgh, my beloved said it was the way salvation might have looked if salvation were anything more than an Impressionist painting hung on a dining room wall. We gaze together at the space where a window should have been.

Law of Parsimony

As I have studied science,
I have studied men & loved them also—
   my cursory diligence, abstracted tenderness:
     in the morning, wake to heresy or sorrow.

It takes me awhile, being back in the world again:
     longings unspooled & artfully rethreaded.

It takes me awhile to remember even this is optional.

But what I admire—
what fetches me time & again to the laboratories
   & the ballfields & the solitary morning strolls
     of Man & Dog or Man with Coffee in Hand & Dog

is the aspiration of both disciples & discipline:
     the science of men, the men of science:
        toward simplicity, precision.

It takes me awhile to remember that mating is no longer required.

I think of the beauty pageant
     when I was only 13, of my mother winding
       my hair over hot-roller sticky-spikes,
       my body shrinking right before our eyes.
         This was Ockham's Razor also.

Shaving my legs until, bare & bony, they bled
     stripping the hair away from my under-arms
       & the tender tops of my toes.

Turning sallow then, my breath tucked in,
    Vaselined teeth & yellowing nails: cut down to size,
     pink lace & white ruffles cuffing me tight,
        scrutiny of a Marriott's worth of strangers.
         This was Ockham's Razor also.

It takes me a while to let the tears drain out of my lungs:
    to breathe again: alive & exonerated.

I think of how it really did look simple on paper:
    a marriage license for 60 bucks & bumming
    a cigarette from the city worker watching the door.

"What d'ya want to get married for?"
      with his scruffy chin & his pretty eyes & his patience,
        waiting for me to reply.

A slew of answers:
    Because it's easier to vote the party line
    Because even cable is never a la carte
    Because I'm a writer: I understand about sentences,
        dependent clauses, conditional & subordinate terms
    And because I have memorized precisely what I am supposed to want
        (They don't call it a steel trap for nothing)

Something about parents & needing to please them, or defy them;
    something about safety & needing to seek it at all costs;
        something about other people understanding that I had been wanted,
        & sought after, earnestly desired.

It takes me awhile to remember, under penalty of perjury, the old Natural Law.

What can be said of the beloved: percussion of her body's praise, deep
    mysterious music that undergirds these syllables but cannot be translated
        into speech: syncopation, improvisation…

And what can be said of the world, with its bristles & Brill-o pads & either/or boxes: that the simplest answer is always the best? that truth can always be calculated, quantified & contained?

What then of desire's capacity to surprise us, of the improbable majesty of the willow-tree & the comforting disquietude of the storm?

The science is impersonal, without eyes. The men are lovely sometimes, but trained the way snipers stalk through the wild: a single target in a circular outline: circumference no greater than a dime...*bull's eye.*

It takes me awhile: to collect myself & my follies & the ivy-twined inquiries of my mind.

It takes me awhile.   She knows this.   In her own intricacy: unabashed & labyrinthine: she sees.

"You can't marry someone when you're in love with someone else."

Though it nearly happened, like a fever sweeping the forehead of every swooning girl. And this time, for once, I wanted to be just like all the others. I knew I could love a man. I was well-practiced in the art of obligation, & I had a curtsy or two left in me from the formative ballet class. I could keep pace with my contemporaries. I could be very good & somewhat graceful. Or I could wash my hands of the whole matter, which is why whenever I tell this story, there's always a prayer hidden somewhere for the man I tried to love & all the ways I failed. There's a joy also, & a primitive sigh: *wife* like an over-plucked string on a tired guitar: but oh, how I yearned to make music! What interests me now is the way we foreshadow our own disappointments, then learn to forget them somehow. When, as a child, I circled the *Ms.* box on my offering envelope, much to my mother's chagrin, & announced proudly—with George Bailey's bravado: "I'm not going to get married, *ever*, to anyone, do you understand? I want to do what *I* want to do." But then I was born again into adolescence, all contested worth & cultish fascination. "Doubt," the Dragon said, "is the only word I trust," & perhaps I trusted also this revision of my wants, this surrender of my secret complications. Like the girls at Catholic School, whose faces I wanted to kiss or crush. Like all the dreams where I turned suddenly male, at odds with myself, for the fleeting brush of a stranger's breast. I wouldn't let the world crack open: *Twilight Zone* or worse—*Twilight of the Golds*. How could I survive, I asked myself, in a world that wished me otherwise, or not at all? But it was still my call: courteous at times & comfortable at others, convenience of the standing date & restlessness of slow receding water. I convinced myself of stunning certainties: the soapbox overturned to pretty pedestal, the promise of a ring that paid for reason. My dress was very white & very straight, sequins & lace & taken in around the waist. I had not been eating much. Too many cigarettes & not enough sleep, coffee by the quart & gin-&-tonics. Until I was sitting one day on the back porch of a best friend's garden apartment, where she was very good at living alone & somewhat graceful at hiding poems she'd rather nobody saw, & I realized I wanted to hold her hand on the Ferris wheel of the future & hear her voice on the intercom of my interior monologue & that I had been, all this time, standing outside myself, becoming the mute carpenter of my grandfather & the manic magician of his daughter, assembling a box with my own two hands in order to make myself of all people disappear. New frost was tender on the blades of grass. Deer crept in from subtle & dramatic distances. If this had been a fairy tale, then I knew at last the forest was listening. A few of the trees had bowed their heads, & a slow admonishing light filtered through the clouds. Illumination came gradually, then indisputably. She whom I loved best, having everything to do with gender & absolutely nothing at all, confessed in a quiet voice to loving me also. "So I guess the old movie was right," despite the fact I was no Captain Von Trapp & my husband-to-be no Baroness Schraeder. And the woman who resembled least of all Fraulein Maria professed the first of our rich history of surprises: "You know," she said, "I've never even seen *The Sound of Music*…"

Double Feature

I. Matinee

Just once I'd like to slink into the dark preamble of the story, hunker down under the spell of soft lights & coming attractions. I'd like to hold my lover's hand & note the lack of reaction from those standing in the aisles & seated on either side. I don't need any NC-17 love scenes, followed by circumspect cigarettes & predictable twists of plot. I don't prefer explosions: TNT or TNA, tea for two & two for tea: musical meets melodrama meets slackening standards of the MPAA. And I don't want to drive all the way downtown to another off-the-hole-in-the-wall cinema just so I can see queer people quipping & fucking & fighting & feeling like I've been somehow restored when mostly I just feel bored & lonely. It's not a mirror of course, our silver screen, but now & then I'd like to tip it slightly askew & see a shadow of myself peeking through. This is how it would be: *Interior, Day*: Two women watching television on a purple couch or arranging bills across a kitchen table. There'd be that sound, a check torn perfectly along its perforation, a sidelong glance, late summer windows crowded with morning glories, or autumn trees stripped slowly in the quickening breeze. What if we simply listened to them talk? What if we simply watched them place their pots & pans into a sink of steaming water? What if their domestic banalities were also our own, small & insignificant & strangely satisfying, like the glisten of a stovetop after scrubbing or the bold aroma of a French-pressed roast? What if there were nothing grand & nothing tragic to culminate their story, to reward or penalize this deviation from the standard, this casual forthright shrug toward the mean? Just once I'd like to find myself embedded in the script, not coming out or going in & nobody *coming to terms*. Just staying home: a character study or an artsy montage or an everyday love affair between two people who just happen to be... An incidental, hardly worth mentioning. As if our chromosomes could possibly contain us, as if—at the end of a long day, in the office, the classroom, the grocery store—it actually mattered whose gendered arm slipped around the gendered waist of whose body to form their silent & contented spoon.

II. Sequel

But of course, it does matter. Your hand, which is a woman's hand, the smooth elongation of your torso, which is a woman's torso, the way our days are not tidy, nor would we have them be. The quotient of entropy—high; the matrix of subtle & insidious presumptions—high; the probability that love is, at least some of the time, a gendered muscle flexing—also high. Sometimes there's a cat on the lap & warm sunshine through the ancient lace curtains: a calyx of our story but not its deep & fractured center, where the petals fall off like plumes along a path no camera lens can follow. We have entered the *beyond* now: beyond flashcards & genre fiction; beyond recipes where each ingredient is listed on the card; beyond sound bytes and soap commercials where the woman stays home with her children, all of whom are always scrubbed so clean as to be nearly polished in a kitchen as bright & white & spacious as a glacier taking its own sweet time across the sea. We don't have that kind of time, & frankly, I'm not all that enamored of domesticity. It's the world I want out sometimes—outing itself as a chamber of forbidden beauties—the *look but don't touch* of them—of sanctified unions & others that pass unnoticed, unacknowledged, unblessed. As if we had never stood in the peat or trudged through the alley to the dented cans… As if we had never weathered a rainstorm or batted our upturned eyes at the lunatic moon, pleading for things we couldn't have…But I come back again to the morning, to the hours unmoored from sleep & the day's runway flecked and glistening with prospects unimagined yet. I come back to my will or to my senses, calling out the old ghosts nestled like birds in the rafters, cooing *emulation*, clucking *simulacrum*, & I resist the false seduction of the un-gendered dreams, the silly parodies & pantomimes of marriage. We are the stuff of montage, pastiche, our little lives still rounded with sleep. Blear-eyed in this dark, before the coffee's on, before the heat is flowing through the house's feeble veins, ye old conundrum: how to seek our feature before we know our name?

Love Poem for Sisyphus

> *To the celestial thunderbolts he preferred the benediction of water.*
> —Camus

As do I, so often: soothing flux of these currents,
soft baptism of this rain; never the sense to come in

out of, now the certainty that life remains
uncertain: the pleasure this brings us, the pain.

O Sisyphus, how you surprise me, man after my own heart:
absurdist hero, friend sought for strength in futile struggle.

Sometimes we cherish in others what we cannot embrace
in ourselves; all this standing water in the well

of consciousness, raising my pail only to pour out
its contents again: & how to distinguish—

repetition from redundancy?
anaphora from tautology?

Sisyphus, you've molded for me a grinding ax,
notching the Tree of Knowledge with heavy

irregular blows. Yes, *you*—servant of
epistemology, your bended knee of bluff

& circumspect camaraderie on our journey
over this river & through these woods

where we cannot be but altered by retracing:
the truth changes, you see—& not just rhetorically,

as when you see in the vanity mirror a new face
set about the same obligations, proceeding in what

would appear the same way. All my life I have strolled
through the sibilant valley, fricative formations

of sex & sleep: how I never go down easily,
clasping climax like a locket at the throat—

anticipating…entropy? longing for…exoneration?
Then the waking, returning of mind to body,

as if an essential eddy, obstructed by stone, has
produced this calm place of contrapuntal motion.

But we best be going again, back to the quarry; sifting
through silt, cutting rock clean away from the hill

only to build it back up: erosion, excavation, reconstruction:
the only tools we have, the only world we know.

Pangaea (4)

    Before   After

    Garden   Fall

       Lost   Found

          Then   Now

(watch how we winnow)

Once upon a time—before the Before, pre-Prelapsaria—

                                        my lines neither

              straightened nor crisscrossed:

                              my heart
                                  not yet bent

                     beyond obedience:

I went fishing with my father.

We sat in a small boat, our knees nearly touching.

The world was our oyster, a bounty of pearls.

We were glad then. Happy as clams.

When the fish tugged my line, I remembered.

We had not come so far for nothing.

Not merely drifting, a day at the sea.

This ritual of lying in wait.

Then the silver fish thrashing, my slackening hands…

                            Reel

            Catch   Hook

Bait   Lure

Roanoke

I will consider changing my name—not the last one,
though—no. I have made my peace with that troubled past,
a promised woman returned to the bridge of unhinged,
water-lilies & lady-watching.   No, I mean
the first name, syllables the cuckold struggles to forget,
pitching his tent, his tongue, in unfamiliar soil.

Bereft of vow & ring, I am no gold star. I am neither
the intricate origami of a map unfolded on the dash, a clash
between two opposing camps—my mother's stilted voice,
my father's sad concern.

Of course I never learn. A footprint in silt. A gash
on the last good tree. Proof of life in the lost colony
of broken limbs & flowers emboldened by sun.
Good-bye was not part of that vernacular. There wasn't time.
A deer hides behind the kilt of jagged roses, persistent even
in autumn, even until the white-capped mountains realign.

We contain our opposites. I kiss your goose-flesh
in the snow. My mother will not let go, even
when the dream dissolves into scream, & the
mirrors must be covered to avoid alarm.

City of other faces;
ancestors foraging for their uncertain lives,
beckoning back to a *simpler time* when
disappearance was common as internal
rhyme.   As Virginia—
which you can call me—if you dare.

Démarche

Open me like a rose;
unburden me of my sweetness.

Till the umber of secrets
with a fervent trowel.

(Rouse me to the trill of your name.)

When all that buttons has been
unbuttoned,

& all that folds has faltered
at the seams,

steam the envelope free from ancient longings.

(Dip your nib in the quick of my flame.)

We Leave the Beaches for the Tourists, Mostly

Brody did not want to believe in the great white any more than the Mayor did. This is the part the history-makers always seem to miss, whenever someone is watching from a crow's nest for land or calling out from a pulpit over the furrowed sand: *EVERYBODY, OUT OF THE WATER!* We want to justify these actions as insight, something we don't have because we are too ordinary, too trusting, like children still singing *Que Sera Sera* in glee club, eating white-bread sandwiches with all the crusts cut off. But Brody had seen the girl, what was left of her, & in the raw terror of that mangled scene, he understood the Cartesian split better than any philosopher. Renouncing it, he might have murmured something, retching into his handkerchief on the lonely drive home to the beach house where his wife & kids were waiting. (In these stories, they are always waiting, as if they never move between frames or step off the stage into someplace unscripted...) Brody might have murmured how the girl did not *have* a body, how some of her parts were not merely *missing*. In fact, Chrissie Watkins *was* a body, the same way his wife was, & his sons, & also himself, which is the hardest moment—the Everyman moment—when the hero understands that flesh is truer than fiction & profit, more trustworthy than any ephemeral soul. And faced with that prospect, what would anyone do? We'd pay the bounty hunter; we'd face our fear of the water. Blood-thirsty, like the enemy, we'd seek our flailing revenge.

The Follower

Because Simon said so, & Simon
was always right, & if you didn't do
as Simon told you to, you could be cast out
of the circle & left to fend for yourself
like birds estranged from their South-flying
flocks, birds that—not knowing better—
had eaten the berries that Simon warned you about,
smashing their bright red bodies against the window
glass, once & again, delirious from the bright red
berries on the prickly bushes with leaves that were
shaped like stars.

Simon, in his infinite wisdom, had cut back
such bushes from the side of the house, exposing
the brick, its red dust & soft white stubble.
But he could do nothing about the stray birds
nesting in the chimney & the attic crawlspace
& the overhead grates where you could see
the tiny tendons of their feet clutching the bars
& their yellow beaks pecking down into the
vacant slipshod dark.

Oh, how they scattered when Simon came
after them, despite his cooing, despite his striking
emulation of their own exceptional sound.
You thought it strange the way humans also
backed away from him as he was talking—
more subtle than the birds, but not so different
in the way obedience resembles a kind of shrinking,
a camera pulling back slowly so the objects in the
foreground are diminished—though, in this version,
the people were the camera & Simon stood
like a tripod (two legs & a cane), unmoving,
as the birds receded & the humans also, & his

aperture trapped only feathered light & fragments
of bodies that did their living beyond the furrowed
reach of his sight.

But Simon said so, & you had to listen, even when
you didn't believe a word anymore; even when he
insisted the birds were carrying terrible messages
scrolled under their feet & homing devices from double
agents across the globe; even when he lamented the loss of
flowers in the ransacked garden (*ransacked*, he called it,
though it was plain to see that winter itself had done
the ravaging); even when you recounted the tale of
Hansel & Gretel—longing in that moment to be
fabled & lost—& Simon said, "Don't you see?
They never found their way home again because the
birds had eaten their foolish trail of crumbs…"

"Skirt the issue."

red wool pinned for safety lest unraveling take place & the plaid promise of the school girl cliché that all is as it should be & is meant to stay pleated skirts & pencil skirts ruffles & dirndls knee-length skirts & circle skirts A-lines & broomsticks mini-skirts maxi-skirts poodle skirts embroidered with prancing cotton-headed dogs & sarongs & culottes & tennis skirts with their irresistible white cotton & tulip-cut skirts & Gibson Girl skirts & corsets & denim & every imaginable anachronism & jersey puffball skirts & flapper skirts complete with fishnet stockings & peacock skirts with fashionable plumage & petticoats suitable for square-dancing & jumpers made of velvet or corduroy & tutus made of transparent tulle & brushed twill riding skirts & diamond-cut calico skirts & Katie skirts Abbie skirts Hampton taffeta suits with matching skirt & jacket & prairie skirts & soft linen Susannah skirts & wrap skirts & cargo skirts with pockets for cigarettes & spare change & ankle-length satin skirts & trouser skirts reversible beach skirts & nylon slips barely long enough to camouflage their garters flamenco skirts & hula skirts & old-fashioned kilts & high-fashion flare & frayed-to-the-fringe leather skirts & bubble skirts & bustled-up Victorian lace skirts willow bark & chain mail skirts & every homemade assemblage of zip & shift including but not limited to the hybrid *skort* & even kayak skirts & saddle skirts & most important of all *bed skirts* which disguise not only the sin of the skin but the place where flesh is most likely to mingle no shortage of skirts & nothing that can't be covered by a simple drape & a few stitches of pliable silk you think you won't be skirted just you wait

Wane

"It's always about something," she claims.
"You can't have a story where nothing happens."

                                              It's about to be winter but

                                      Zeno's Paradox suggests

                        winter (so-called) will never arrive.

     What does that mean

                    for the leaves   for the trees

        legions of them—   unshaken   unstirred?

Maybe it's a story about pilgrims: ordinary people   agnostic, afraid.

                      (Does penance have to have a purpose?)

                                                It's about to be
                                         my mother's birthday.

"All right," I confess. "I've never been to Confession.
Well, once. Almost.

I told someone else's story. I lied."

"What did you say had happened?"

"That my parents died, in a car crash, like Pollyanna's."

                She thinks it was a train.
                Does it matter?

Maybe it's a story about orphans then: ordinary people
                                      agnostic, afraid.

                        It's about to be Christmas but

                        Zeno's Paradox suggests

                        Christmas (so-called) will never arrive.

            What does that mean

                    for the cloud-silt & the snow-salt,

        the sideways slant of torrid sea-rain?

"Pluto used to be a planet. I remember so well.
My Very Exceptional Mother Just Served Us Nine Pizzas."

    "Were you always fond of mnemonics?"

"No. But I get lonely now, when I look at the night sky."

        (Isn't science a story too?)

Maybe it's really a story about pirates—
how they earn a living when the bounty hunting's bad.
Shoveling driveways. Scraping windshields.
Selling, if it comes to that, their own blood.

        It's about to be 20 years since

        I couldn't go home again.

        Zeno's Paradox suggests

        I (so-called) can never go back.

"When the priest was done, he told me,
'Go say 10 Hail Marys.' I only ever said three."

    "What were you waiting for?"

The snowman, melting, with the derelict eyes.

The picturebook comprised of piecharts.

The grandfather to tuck me in & whisper *Goodnight Moon*.

Check the wall-clock with

the one bad hand.

The cop shouts, "Stick 'em up!"

The gambler calls, "Fold."

The sleeper knows

it's about to be

mo(u)rning.

Pangaea (5)

…teach them to long for the endless immensity of the sea…

        to surpass petty pageantries
                      of conquest

                                & love extravagantly

                to revel in their impeccable geotropic design

        teach them the fragile certitude of starfish

& these pleasures—

                mystery   melancholy   surprise

                wrap them in a cool chrysalis of knowing:

  porous as flesh,

    delicate as parchment:

        on which may be etched that fateful message-in-the-bottle

          from which may be launched that fateful ship

                                               & the passengers come

                           later than promised, empty-handed or

              with tickets crumpled in longing, corsages askew:

teach them the performance of beauty, the breaking of bread—

                               symmetries split like the starboard veil

The Opaque Dilemma of Daylight

I said to myself, "It will be a dark poem,"
as if this imprecise color—*dark*—were able to capture,
or clearly imply, my prevailing sense of impediment.

Then, I thought of Sisyphus,
as I often do—how it seems to be his motion I crave:
pushing the stone uphill, chasing the boulder back down.

For Sisyphus, of course, the path is clear; his impediment
moves with him; he is not *obstructed* as such. Rather,
condemned to a knowable fate, a sparkling translucence.

This story, this Sisyphus, is not a dark poem.
Tragic perhaps, but lit by the soft lamps of
gusto & verve.

Now what of the still point?
What of the still point in the turning world?

Beleaguered by winter, battered by snow,
I feel myself transfixed into axis: intersection
of lines, contradictory desires: motionless

in the flecked cold's accumulation,
the slanted gales of wind.

When Angie says, "We must be trudging
through the ugliest snow globe in the world,"
I laugh & dust my mittens.

At the corner's dense impediment of traffic,
buses yawn & growl, snaking through pedestrian sprawl
like trowels through a thick layer of soil.

Soon, the radio reports, we may see "white-out
conditions": eclipses of light by light. Not *dark*—
this blizzard of mixed imperatives, fraught blessings.

I am a little girl in galoshes, a little girl with a note
pinned to her coat from a teacher who writes in
her best grown-up penmanship:

"The student is sensitive. The student suffers
from extreme sensitivity to light."

The little girl never imagines she will be standing
here—on this wilted corner, in this white-washed city:
this *Opacity*: lacking Sisyphean strength, lacking

Sisyphean leverage—and leverage, it must be stated,
is among the most terrible things to lack—

A grown-up girl, with deep treads in her boots
& dim stars in her eyes, still waiting
for the light to change.

The Cartographer

She represents a "diminished demographic." That's what they tell her at the Young Professionals Lunch. "Do you ever work free-lance?" "Do you ever draw free-hand?" "What does a cartographer *do* in her spare time?" The woman is patient. The woman is private. She lets them speculate about her childhood, her interest in blueprints, her failed attempts at architecture. Was she the kind of girl who always brought maps to Show & Tell? Did her father collect globes? Was her mother unhappy? But I have only one question—Can she help me? *Will* she? The woman is patient. She listens with her eyes. She traces the rim of a white ceramic coffee cup with the tip of her nimble finger. What I want to know is, when you draw a door, does it materialize? When you paint gridlines on a piece of ordinary paper, do people begin to fit into pre-apportioned places? And what about the seats on airplanes, the lack of legroom and the short-but-infinite distance between Coach & First Class? The woman is patient. The woman confesses she has never traveled much. What I want to know is, are there maps that haven't been drawn yet? Are there new shortcuts slated to emerge in the next 10-15 years? New neighborhoods? New civilizations? Outer Space is one thing, I think; leave it to the astronauts, the celestial cartographers & theologians. But I am desperately—and here I might have even touched her thin & veiny hand—desperately concerned about the Inner. The woman is gentle. She doesn't speak much & looks down when she answers. What I want to know is, how fixed is time? Is it fixed as the line on the page, or might there be some way to maneuver around it, some secret corridor she could sketch as a transversal, slicing sideways across the Past & Future—which don't touch, you know, despite assertions to the contrary. The woman is patient. She thinks a long time before rising for a refill. What I want to know is, can I walk backwards down the cobbled road of WHAT HAPPENED, can I climb over the garden wall of WHAT COULD BE STILL, can I cut swiftly through the lingonberry fields before the first birth of the first member of my family & negotiate a moment with the clergyman milking his cow, trimming his roses? What I want to know is, what I want to know is—topographically speaking—how deep is the earth, how wide is the heart, how possible my small & only life?

Requiem for the White Bluff Watch Dog

Because Bull was a big strong mutt kept for company
& running coyotes off into the thick night—a linebacker-
necked sasquatch of a dog who could growl a good one but
never meant anyone harm. His job was simple: guiding
Charlene out to the barn & back so the horses got fed;
holing up under the house at the first slap of thunder or a
lightning-crack; panting for Angie on the porch late nights
humid & heavy with smoke; frightening the FedEx man
when he chanced his rickety white rig down the unpaved
perfidy of Anthony Lane; & most importantly—sprawling out
under the bright banner of Tennessee stars, wallowing in
moonlight, decadent in his own mixed-blood, flea-ridden
bag of glorious bones.

    I was the first Yankee he ever knew, & he didn't
hold it against me: bless him for that, & for those damp eyes
dry of all suspicion, that mighty gray tongue sloppy & sincere,
that untrained tail that couldn't stop its twitching as he welcomed me—
wet nose over burred paw over raggedy ear—out of the car, into the
moon-shine, a stranger there, to the crickets' fury & the roosters' wail,
& the fog that floats like some god shed its clothes.

Détente

I think of you now,

        knowing we are as we must be—

knowing you are not one woman

        or one man, but a collage of bodies—

passed over, slipped under, seen through

And I want you

        to think of me in this collective way also—

to blush on a bridge in cold weather, imagining my hand;

        & again, under awnings, in the cinematic rain—

conjuring my purple umbrella

Once, which is a sapling bent early in storm—

        thereafter, which is long & unremitting, permanent

surpassing transitory, making old our new; mornings I plead

        I'm sorry to the wind, to the dogs in heat, to the harvest

of my own good life, my plebeian heart.

Reading Robinson Crusoe Again, for the Last Time

Your whole life, you learn a language. Before you begin to speak,
you understand what is being spoken. Before you begin to touch,
you possess a tacit knowledge of the surface of things. In time,
you learn what will burn you (stove), what will comfort you (blanket).
You sense who you can trust. You build small walls around the garden
of all that is precious, all that you hold dear. You carry the memory with
you, as you grow older, of what it means to be safe & happy & young.

After all, you too were born in a given year in a certain land & to a good
family. You did not imagine being stranded, separated from the ones who
were once like you, who you were once like. You did not imagine all the
words you would no longer speak, all the voices that would no longer
answer. You did not imagine the tricks your mind would play when faced
with such vastness—island so remote, the social nature of the human creature
of which you are still (& always) one.

Crusoe too was privileged. Crusoe too imposed his mastery & wielded
his will. But for you, there is no returning to the world of your childhood.
One could argue, as Wolfe once did, the same is true for everyone. No going
back again, no going home. But here your stories begin to diverge.
You have taken no prisoners. You have slaughtered no one, rescued no one.
You have not read the Bible in many years, though you have experienced
a conversion of sorts, an opening out of yourself onto a world that cannot
embrace you—not now, in your traitorous entirety—you, child it once
considered its own.

Correspondence is restricted on the island. Crusoe, after 28 years, returned
to the mainland, married, fathered three children, went on as he had been—
restored, in a sense, if also altered. What of those words he began to lose on
the island? Did he recover them? Were they waiting, as they always had been:
the cliff-side stone poised with potential, patient until keenly deployed?

For you, exile is essential, eternal. You are no longer a citizen of your birthplace—
the Straits of—but now its full name escapes you. Let us call it simply The Straits.
Some will swim out to meet you; others will sail past & away. And the island

has become its own kind of paradise. There is love there, with its burns & comforts. Your hungers are sated, your longings quelled. Sometimes you question why you didn't wreck sooner; often, you are grateful for this phantom shore, these sentinel stars; for the freedom to send up your flare or linger there, in the quiet lap of the inter-tide.

You once understood unanimity. Now you know best anonymity. Amity & enmity have been reversed in places. The ones you loved best know the least about you. A stranger is as true a friend as a friend, perhaps truer. You are not sure if you are missed. You are not certain your absence matters now, or if your presence would change it. Where once you were unmistakable, now you are easily overlooked, superimposed onto unfamiliar stories. Every day you wake with this burden: no one will ever find you, unless you choose to be found.

"There's no hole on earth where the heart drops through without bringing something with it."

Despite its long affiliation with loss, love also accrues: steady accumulation of boxes no longer reserved for shoes; strange tinctures & hollow rings, powdered with sugar or stronger; Kewpie dolls won in dart games & a dozen Trivial Pursuits, series of subsequent editions. And the luggage & the tickets & the key-chain souvenirs, all figurative of course: also fashionable & forward-looking & fact. You don't journey alone anymore. There is someone else to think of, to offer the window seat to—or perhaps she prefers the aisle. A twin bed looks suddenly lonely, & more so the large bed, bereft of multiple bodies. Your pillow adopts her scent; your blankets no longer yours. The whole world pluraled, this second pulse shadowing your own. Old companions less companionable: radio, television—mere background noise. You begin to hear her voice reciting the grocery list or answering the phone. There is an attention to content but also to form. You form your syllables with her presence in mind, tailored to the shape of her body. You anticipate her wishes, her kisses, the warm place she has been sitting, wrapped in one of her sweaters with burly wood buttons & in-folded sleeves. You wonder if you are becoming transparent, if she can always see through you to the seed of your truest intention. Will she warm her hands on the low fire you always keep burning, clandestine & solely for her? Will you remain astonished by her luminous capacities: for pleasure, for penance & pardon? There is with her & without her but never beyond. She has altered your constitution. You find her in miniature & metonym: pretty crescents of her thumbnails, velveteen lobes of her ears. You can no longer watch *Jeopardy!* in solitude. Marlboro Lights & lucky bamboo trigger visceral reminiscences. And the tatters on your map, torn together: Rapid City, South Dakota, Niagara Falls, Mount Shasta's surreal setting sun. You remember bookcases in Nancy Drew stories, how they almost always hid the mystery stairs. She has passed through those passageways now; she has found your counterfeit copy of *Great Expectations* & tipped it just so, exposing the secret room. And the safe behind the picture with the traveling eyes, & the skeleton key sequestered in the flower pot, & all that spare change lining the sofa cushions. Not piracy or bribery, but a deep & unencumbered knowing. You have climbed into the hold together. You have sifted through the treasure. And each day past, & every day forward, you have crossed your hearts & murmured something about honor. You have ridden bicycles with cross-hatched baskets stuffed to brimming with roses—all figurative of course: also tender & romantic & accurate beyond accounting. There have been no altars, no trains & veils, but thresholds crossed with kindness & tokens whose meanings exceed the scope of words. You have handled handkerchiefs & checkbooks & gold pocket-watches, meting out an uncertain number of hours. You have made public parables & private apologies. You have swept chimneys & taken out the ash. You have stood together on the fire escape of a condemned building. You have crossed your hearts & promised not to die.

About the Author

Julie Marie Wade's previous collections include *Wishbone: A Memoir in Fractures*, *Small Fires: Essays*, *Postage Due: Poems & Prose Poems*, *When I Was Straight*, *SIX*, *Same-Sexy Marriage: A Novella in Poems*, and *Just an Ordinary Woman Breathing*. With Denise Duhamel, she wrote *The Unrhymables: Collaborations in Prose*, and with Brenda Miller, *Telephone: Essays in Two Voices*. A winner of the Marie Alexander Poetry Series and the Lambda Literary Award for Lesbian Memoir, Wade teaches in the creative writing program at Florida International University and reviews regularly for *Lambda Literary Review* and *The Rumpus*. A Seattle native, she now makes her home in Dania Beach with Angie Griffin and their two cats.

About The Word Works

Since its founding in 1974, The Word Works has steadily published volumes of contemporary poetry and presented public programs. Its imprints include The Washington Prize, The Tenth Gate Prize, The Hilary Tham Capital Collection, and International Editions.

Monthly, The Word Works offers free literary programs in the Chevy Chase, MD, Café Muse series, and each summer it holds free poetry programs in Washington, D. C.'s Rock Creek Park. Word Works programs have included "In the Shadow of the Capitol," a symposium and archival project on the African American intellectual community in segregated Washington, D.C.; the Gunston Arts Center Poetry Series; the Poet Editor panel discussions at The Writer's Center; Master Class workshops; and a writing retreat in Tuscany, Italy.

As a 501(c)3 organization, The Word Works has received awards from the National Endowment for the Arts, the National Endowment for the Humanities, the D.C. Commission on the Arts & Humanities, the Witter Bynner Foundation, Poets & Writers, The Writer's Center, Bell Atlantic, the David G. Taft Foundation, and others, including many generous private patrons.

An archive of artistic and administrative materials in the Washington Writing Archive housed in the George Washington University Gelman Library. It is a member of the Community of Literary Magazines and Presses and its books are distributed by Small Press Distribution.

wordworksbooks.org

OTHER WORD WORKS BOOKS

Annik Adey-Babinski, *Okay Cool No Smoking Love Pony*
Karren L. Alenier, *Wandering on the Outside*
Karren L. Alenier, ed., *Whose Woods These Are*
Karren L. Alenier & Miles David Moore, eds.,
    Winners: A Retrospective of the Washington Prize
Christopher Bursk, ed., *Cool Fire*
Willa Carroll, *Nerve Chorus*
Grace Cavalieri, *Creature Comforts*
Abby Chew, *A Bear Approaches from the Sky*
Nadia Colburn, *The High Shelf*
Henry Crawford, *The Binary Planet*
Barbara Goldberg, *Berta Broadfoot and Pepin the Short*
Akua Lezli Hope, *Them Gone*
Frannie Lindsay, *If Mercy*
Elaine Maggarrell, *The Madness of Chefs*
Marilyn McCabe, *Glass Factory*
Kevin McLellan, *Ornitheology*
JoAnne McFarland, *Identifying the Body*
Leslie McGrath, *Feminists Are Passing from Our Lives*
Ann Pelletier, *Letter That Never*
Ayaz Pirani, *Happy You Are Here*
W.T. Pfefferle, *My Coolest Shirt*
Jacklyn Potter, Dwaine Rieves, Gary Stein, eds.,
    Cabin Fever: Poets at Joaquin Miller's Cabin
Robert Sargent, *Aspects of a Southern Story*
    & *A Woman from Memphis*
Julia Story, *Spinster for Hire*
Julie Marie Wade, *Skirted*
Miles Waggener, *Superstition Freeway*
Fritz Ward, *Tsunami Diorama*
Camille-Yvette Welsh, *The Four Ugliest Children in Christendom*
Amber West, *Hen & God*
Maceo Whitaker, *Narco Farm*
Nancy White, ed., *Word for Word*